Why Do I Laugh or Cry?

and other questions about the nervous system

by

Sharon Cromwell

Photographs by

Richard Smolinski, Jr.

Series Consultant

Dan Hogan

RIGBY INTERACTIVE LIBRARY
DES PLAINES, ILLINOIS

© 1998 Reed Educational & Professional Publishing
Published by Rigby Interactive Library,
an imprint of Reed Educational & Professional Publishing,
1350 East Touhy Avenue, Suite 240 West
Des Plaines, IL 60018

02 01 00 99 98
10 9 8 7 6 5 4 3 2 1

Produced by Times Offset (M) Sdn. Bhd.

Library of Congress Cataloging-in-Publication Data

Cromwell, Sharon, 1947-
    Why do I laugh or cry? : and other questions about the nervous system / by Sharon Cromwell ; photographs by Richard Smolinski, Jr.
       p. cm. -- (Body wise)
    Includes bibliographical references and index.
    Summary: Describes how the human nervous system works and discusses such related topics as goose bumps, blushing, and dreaming.
    ISBN 1-57572-161-9 (lib. bdg.)
    1. Nervous system--Juvenile literature. [1. Nervous system.]
I. Smolinski, Dick, ill. II. Title. III. Series.
QP361.5.C76 1998
612.8--dc21
                                        97-25172
                                             CIP
                                             AC

Some words are shown in bold, **like this**. You can find out what they mean by looking in the glossary.

3/99

Contents

What is my nervous system?

Every day you have **experiences.** You have them whether you are at home, at school, or on a trip. Some make you laugh. Some make you worried. Some take you by surprise. How does your body receive all this information from these experiences? It is all processed by your nervous system.

The main parts of your nervous system are your brain, spinal cord, and nerves. Your brain and spinal cord are your central nervous system. Your nerves go to all parts of your body. Some of them—the thickest ones—are attached to your spinal cord. The top of your spinal chord is attached to the lowest part of your brain.

Your nerves carry messages at lightning speed from one part of your body to another. Each nerve is made of tiny nerve cells, or neurons. Your body has billions of neurons. Most of them are in your brain.

HEALTH FACT
When you're well rested, your nerves can send messages at top speed.

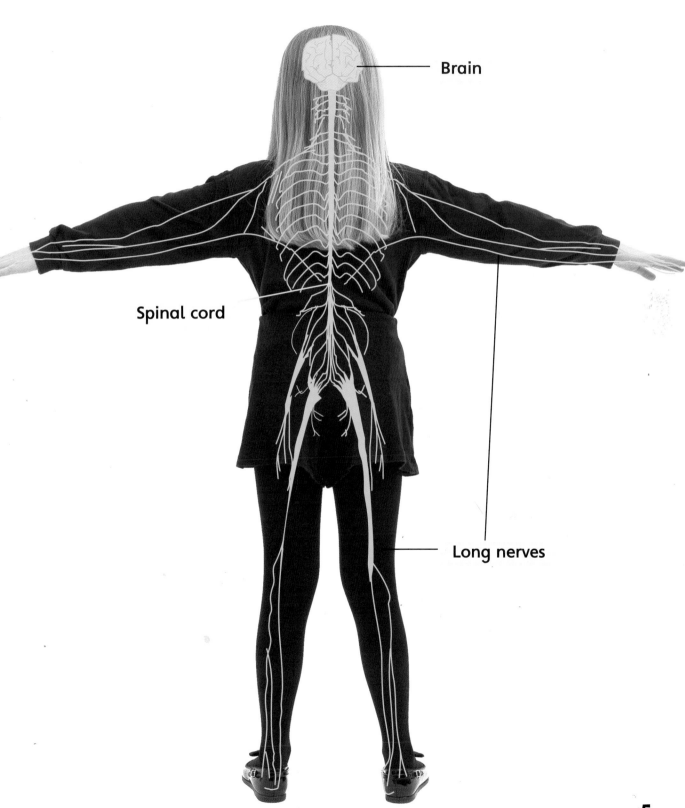

Brain

Spinal cord

Long nerves

How do my nerves help me?

Some neurons carry messages from your sense **organs**—such as your eyes and ears. These are sensory neurons. When you see or hear something, your sense organs send tiny electrical signals through your neurons to your brain. Your brain then identifies the object or the sound.

Other neurons in your brain send signals through long nerves in your arms and legs to the neurons that are attached to your muscles. The neurons that help you move are motor neurons. When you want to walk, your brain sends signals to motor neurons in your legs. Those neurons tell your leg muscles to move. Sometimes your motor neurons tell your leg muscles to pull away from something sharp—such as a piece of broken glass.

HEALTH FACT

If you have a deep cut, be sure to show it to an adult. You may need to see a doctor.

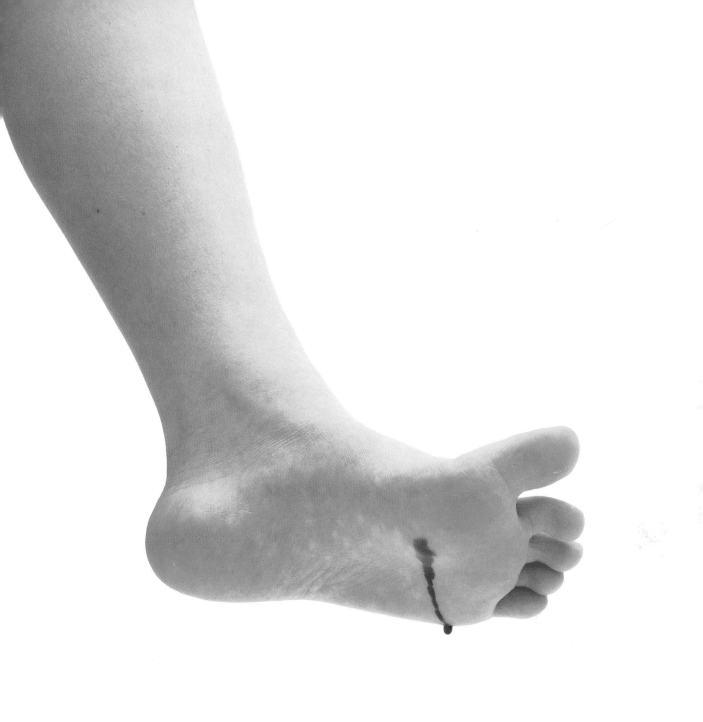

Why do I forget some things?

Memories are made and stored when your brain forms a new path made from connections between your neurons. This memory returns every time nerve signals pass along this same path of neuron connections. This is how you record and store all kinds of information and **experiences** in your brain.

HEALTH FACT

You can make up rhymes or other clues to help yourself remember things, such as someone's name. The name *Dan*, for example, rhymes with the word *man*.

1. You create a memory by making a new path of neuron connections. You can make this path in many parts of your brain.

2. These new paths of neuron connections create something like a video recording that your brain plays back as a memory.

3. Some paths, like remembering your name or how to tie your shoes, are made to last for a long time. These form your long-term memory.

4. Other paths, like memorizing lines in a play, are needed for only a short time. These connections form your short-term memory.

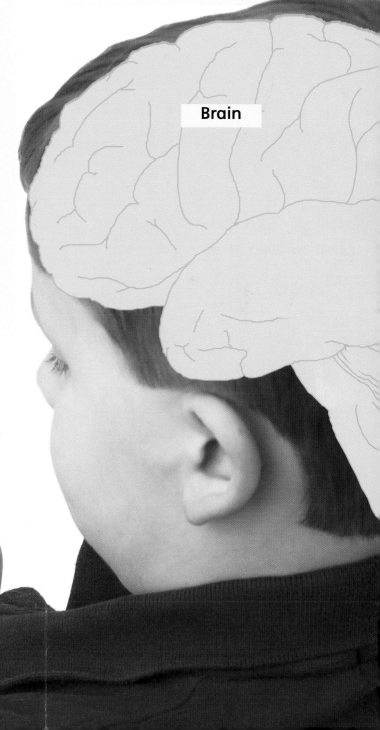

Brain

Why do I laugh and cry?

Your emotions are affected by many different natural **chemicals** in your body. Your brain controls these chemicals.

1. Sometimes you see or hear something funny. Other times you see or hear something sad.

2. When you see or hear something, neurons in your eyes or ears send a message along your nerves to your brain.

3. This message triggers the release of a chemical that either makes you feel happy or sad.

4. If enough of the chemical is released, it may also send a message to your face that either makes you laugh or makes you cry.

Brain

11

Why does my face feel hot and turn a darker color when I'm embarrassed?

When you're embarrassed, a **chemical** is released in your body. When your brain senses this chemical, it sends a message to the tiny blood vessels in the skin of your face. It tells them to get wider. This sends a rush of blood to your skin and makes your face feel warm and turn red. Blushing is a kind of reflex reaction. A reflex reaction is something you can't control. You do it before you have time to think about it.

HEALTH FACT
Everybody blushes, but differences in skin color can hide blushing in some people.

1. You see, feel, or hear something that embarrasses you.

2. A chemical is released.

3. Your brain quickly sends messages to tiny blood vessels in the skin of your face. Blood vessels are tiny, thin tubes that carry blood.

4. The blood vessels in your face get wider and fill with more blood.

5. The extra blood in the blood vessels makes your face turn a redder or darker color.

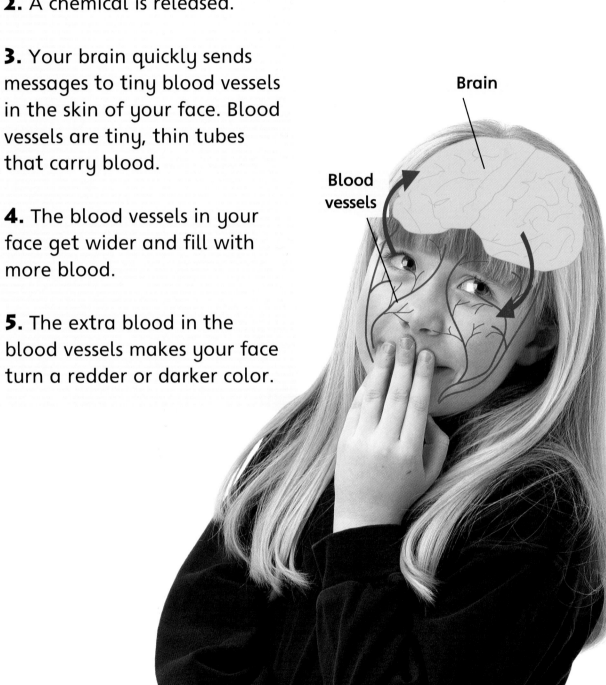

Brain

Blood vessels

Why does my tongue pull away when I taste something hot?

Sensory neurons in your tongue send a message that goes to your spinal cord. If you are tasting or touching something dangerously hot, your spinal cord will order your motor neurons to tell your tongue or hand to pull away. This is another kind of reflex reaction. Your body reacts to these dangers instantly, before you are even aware of them.

HEALTH FACT
If you burn yourself, quickly put the burned area of your body under cold, running water. This will make the burn less painful.

1. When your tongue touches very hot food, sensory neurons carry the message right to the spinal cord.

2. A part of the spinal cord gives orders to motor neurons. They take the message and tell your tongue to pull away from the food.

3. The message does not go to the brain first, so you don't think about what's happening.

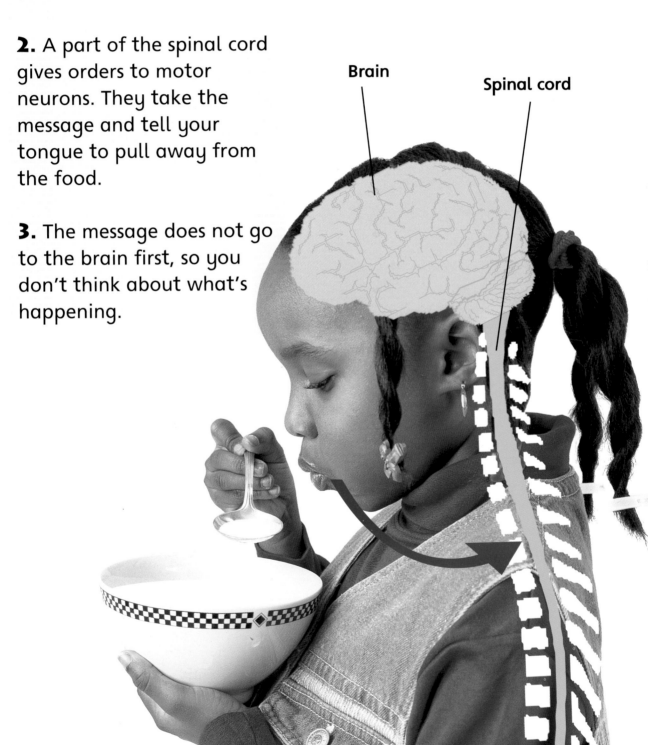

Brain

Spinal cord

Why do I feel goose bumps all over my skin when I'm nervous?

You get goose bumps all over your body when your nerves trigger the release of a **chemical** called a hormone.

HEALTH FACT

Calcium (an important mineral in dairy products) has a naturally calming effect on the nervous system.

1. When you are uneasy or frightened, your brain sends messages to several body parts called glands. Glands make chemicals called hormones.

2. The glands release a certain kind of hormone all through your body.

3. The hormone affects different parts of your body, including certain muscles in the skin of your arms and legs. When these muscles contract, the hairs on your arms and legs stand up, and small bumps form on the skin.

4. Even though an uneasy feeling seems to start with these goose bumps, it is really your nervous system and your hormones at work.

Brain

Gland

Glands

Why do smells make me remember things?

Just as your brain creates memories from things you see or hear, smells also cause your brain to create sensory recordings. Sometimes, the smell memory is recorded at the same time as a seeing or hearing memory.

HEALTH FACT

Pleasant smells, such as the smell of a rose or of the ocean, often make us feel good.

1. Of all your senses, smell has the shortest and most direct pathway to your hippocampus.

2. Your hippocampus is one part of your brain that creates memories.

3. Because your sense of smell has such a strong and direct connection to your hippocampus, smells will often trigger memories.

4. Your sense of smell is also closely connected to your limbic system. Your limbic system is the center of feelings and emotions in your brain. That's why a familiar smell may trigger memories that make you feel sad or happy.

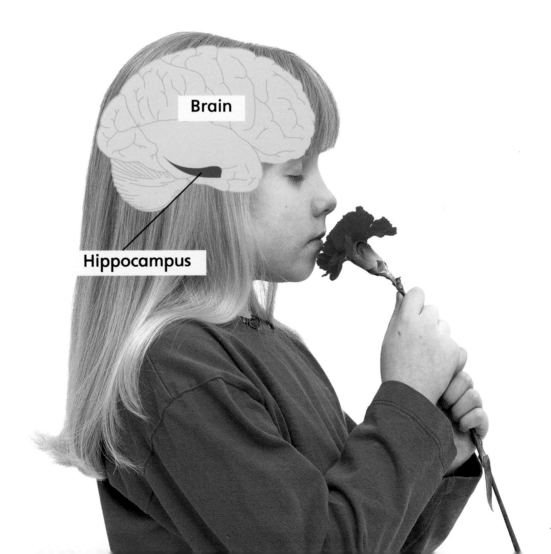

Brain

Hippocampus

Why do I dream?

The answers to many questions about dreaming are still a mystery. Most researchers believe that while you sleep, your brain needs to replay and organize the memories it has recorded.

HEALTH FACT
Children between the ages of 5 and 9 need between 10 and 11 hours of sleep.

1. Your senses and motor system have little to do while you sleep. While these systems are resting, your brain stays active with the memories it has recorded.

2. Researchers believe that your brain is constantly organizing the memories and information it has stored. Sometimes these memories are about something that happened to you during the day. Other times, they may be experiences you had years ago.

3. Sometimes, your dreams mix old memories with new ones. Suppose you dream about a new school. In this new school is a boy you haven't seen for a very long time. In the dream, your brain has made certain nerve cell connections that have tied a new memory (your new school) to an old one (your memory of the boy).

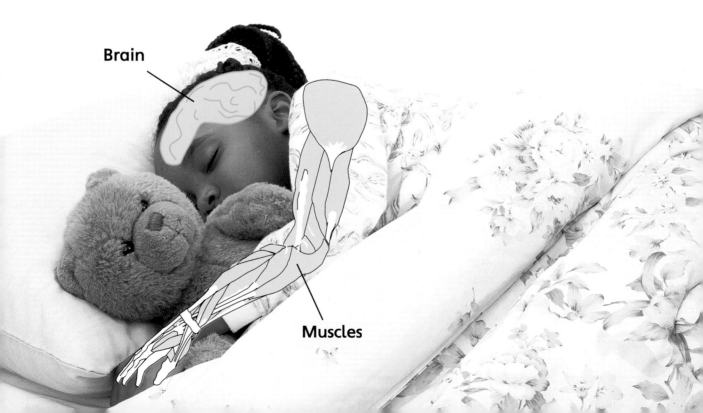

Brain

Muscles

EXPLORE MORE!
Your Nervous System

1. STARRING ROLE!

WHAT YOU'LL NEED:

- a book or play
- a friend to help you

THEN TRY THIS!

You have two kinds of memory: long-term and short-term. This activity will show you a little bit about how your memory works.

Pick a small section out of a book or play. It should be about 15–20 lines long. Read it over carefully twice, then put it down. Try to say out loud the exact words you just read. Your friend can read along silently. Then read through the passage another two times. Put it down and try to say the words out loud again. How much better are you the second time? This uses your short-term memory.

Read the passage once more. Then come back to it after a week. Try to recite the passage. How much can you remember? Whatever you remember has probably made it into your long-term memory!

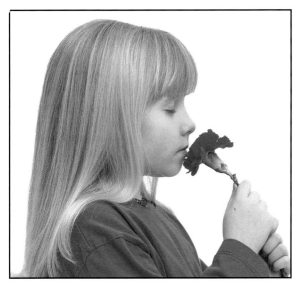

2. ODOR DECODER!
WHAT YOU'LL NEED:
- a sheet of paper and pencil
- 3 to 5 different foods with strong smells

THEN TRY THIS!
Close your eyes and hold one of the foods under your nose. Take a deep breath in.
Does the smell make you remember anything? Write your memories and thoughts on the sheet of paper. Then do the same thing with the other foods.

When you finish, read what you've written on the paper. Then think of other smells that make you remember people, places, or things.

3. DREAM TEAM!
WHAT YOU'LL NEED:
- sheet of paper and pencil

THEN TRY THIS!
See if you can figure out what some of your dreams mean.

Put your pencil and paper by your bed. For three mornings in a row, as soon as you wake up, write about your dreams on the sheet of paper. After three days, sit down and read through the dreams again. Are any dreams similar? Different? Can you think of something that happened to you that might have caused a dream?

Glossary

chemicals In this book, chemicals are substances that your body makes. These substances can make you feel happy, sad, or embarrassed.

experiences Things that happen to you.

organs Parts of the body that do one job.

More Books to Read

Bennett, David. *What Am I Made of?* New York: Simon & Schuster Childrens, 1991.

Carratello, Pat. *Body Basics.* Westminster, CA: Teacher Created Materials, 1987.

LeMaster, Leslie J. *Your Brain and Nervous System.* Danbury, CT: Childrens Press, 1984.

Parker, Steve. *The Brain and Nervous System.* Danbury, CT: Franklin Watts, 1990.

Silverstein, Alvin. *The Nervous System.* New York: 21st Century Books, 1994.

Index